WILLIAM PENN

Founder of Pennsylvania

BY **Steven Kroll**

ILLUSTRATED BY
Ronald Himler

Holiday House / New York

ACKNOWLEDGEMENT

The author would like to thank Andrew Shankman, Assistant Professor of History, Grand Valley State University, for his valuable assistance.

Library of Congress Cataloging-in-Publication Data

Kroll, Steven.
William Penn, founder of Pennsylvania / by Steven Kroll;
illustrated by Ronald Himler. — 1st ed.
p.   cm.
Summary: A biography of William Penn, founder of the Quaker colony
of Pennsylvania, who struggled throughout his life for the freedom
to practice his religion.
ISBN 0-8234-1439-6
1. Penn, William, 1644–1718—Juvenile literature.   2. Pioneers—
Pennsylvania—Biography—Juvenile literature.   3. Quakers—
Pennsylvania—Biography—Juvenile literature.   4. Pennsylvania—
History—Colonial period, ca. 1600–1775—Juvenile literature.
[1. Penn, William, 1644–1718.   2. Quakers.   3. Pennsylvania—
History—Colonial period, ca. 1600–1775.]
I. Himler, Ronald, ill.   II. Title.
F152.2.K76   2000
974.8'02'092—dc21
[B]   98-18932
CIP   AC

For Ellen Mager,
who insisted
S. K.

Born to a life of privilege, William Penn chose dissent instead. In a turbulent time, when breaking from the established Church of England could mean imprisonment and even death, William became a Quaker. Seeking religious freedom for himself and other Quakers, he founded Pennsylvania with the goal of tolerance for everyone. In and out of jail all his life, he never abandoned his principles.

Charles I

Oliver Cromwell

William Penn spent his whole life caught up in the great events of history. When he was born, on October 14, 1644, a civil war was being fought in England. King Charles I was on one side, and Parliament and religious dissenters called Puritans were on the other. Penn's father, William Penn, a captain in the British navy, was torn. He wanted to be loyal to the king, but Oliver Cromwell, the leader of the Puritans, had taken over the navy. So Captain Penn was fighting in the service of Cromwell when he rushed home for his son's birth. Shortly thereafter he became a rear admiral.

Living in filthy, crowded London, young William caught smallpox at age three but survived. Taking no more chances, the admiral moved his family to a country house in Wanstead. Still, there was no escaping the political situation, which grew steadily more grim.

In 1649, Cromwell and the Puritans finally won the civil war. Cromwell became Lord Protector of the Commonwealth and had the king beheaded. The king's son, Charles II, fled to Holland.

In 1655, Cromwell granted Admiral Penn an estate in Ireland called Macroom. That same year William, age eleven, entered Chigwell Free Grammar School, where he studied Latin and Greek and learned that one did not have to observe religious rituals to be truly religious. He also experienced an inner peace—and discovered God.

In August 1656, the Penn family moved to Macroom. The following year the admiral invited Thomas Loe, a member of The Religious Society of Friends, also known as the Quakers, to the castle.

The Quaker movement was only ten years old, but laws were already being passed against it. Nevertheless, Loe preached powerfully of the belief in an Inner Light and in man's ability to communicate directly with God. He also spoke of plain, honest living, equality, pacifism, and freedom of conscience. William was deeply moved.

In 1658, Oliver Cromwell died. When the monarchy was restored in 1660, Admiral Penn found favor with the new king, Charles II, and was knighted. Later that year, his son became a student at Christ Church College, Oxford University.

In his second year at Oxford, William began attending lectures at the home of Dr. John Owen, a Puritan preacher who encouraged tolerance and individual thought. William refused to attend the required Church of England services at Oxford. He was expelled in March 1662.

His father sent him to Paris, where William stepped into the elegant world of the royal court. But Loe's and Owen's teachings stayed with him. Disturbed by the court's superficiality, he left Paris to study with Moses Amyraut, a well-respected Protestant professor who taught him more about religious liberty and freedom of conscience.

Stylish and more mature, William returned to London in August 1664 and began legal training at Lincoln's Inn. Then, in June 1665, the Great Plague struck the city. Quakers were still being persecuted, but William saw those same Quakers offering help to the dying as the nobility fled.

The Penns' Irish estate, Macroom, had been restored to its original owner, but now Sir William was given land around Cork Harbor and below Kinsale. He sent young William over to help with the tenants. While in Ireland, William again heard Thomas Loe preach. Everything he had learned about religion came together in his mind. He became a Quaker.

By 1668, young William was preaching Quakerism. When he wrote *The Sandy Foundation Shaken,* a tract attacking belief in the Trinity, he was arrested and thrown into the Tower of London on December 2. While there he wrote *No Cross, No Crown,* defending belief in one God and calling for an end to religious persecution.

Eight months later, William's father got him released and sent him back to Ireland so he'd stay out of trouble. On the way, William hired Philip Ford as his business manager.

When William arrived back in London in 1670, the country was in the middle of another religious struggle. King Charles II was trying to move toward toleration of Catholicism. Parliament, working against the king again, passed laws restricting religious groups other than the Church of England from meeting and preaching. On August 14, William boldly preached outside the barred door of the Gracechurch Street Meetinghouse.

He and William Mead, a London dry-goods dealer, were arrested and imprisoned at the foul Black Dog Inn in Newgate Market. Their trial raised important questions about civil liberties in England.

Because Quakers feel *all* people should be treated equally, Penn and Mead refused to remove their hats in court. They were fined for contempt. Then the jury was fined for contempt when it wouldn't find the two men guilty. A year later it was decided that a jury could not be punished for its verdict. Meanwhile Sir William, ill and dying, paid the fines for Mead and young William, and they were released.

But William could not be silenced. Five months later he was back in Newgate Prison for unlawful assembly and refusal to swear an oath against taking up arms against the king. Freed after six months, he went off to organize Quaker meetings in Holland and Germany. Upon his return, after what had been a four-year courtship, he married Gulielma Springett, stepdaughter of the well-known Quaker Isaac Penington, on April 4, 1672.

The laws against religious freedom were growing even stricter in England. William and the other Quaker leaders realized that they needed to find a place where they would be free from persecution. For some time, the Quakers had been interested in establishing a colony in America. Quaker settlers had begun arriving in west New Jersey in 1675, but with land available across the Delaware River, another outpost seemed a good idea.

William applied for a land grant on June 1, 1680, but didn't receive the final Charter that made him Absolute Proprietor of Pennsylvania—"Penn's Woods"—until March 4, 1681. Officially William got the grant because the king owed his father a large debt for loans and services, but more likely than not, the Crown had become interested in getting rid of more Quakers.

William and the First Adventurers, as the Quakers who joined him were called, approved the *Frame of Government* for Pennsylvania in the spring of 1682. A Provincial Council and General Assembly were set up—the Council to make the laws and the larger Assembly to approve them. There would be free elections, trial by jury, and freedom of religion.

Shortly before his departure for America, William signed a bill from his manager, Philip Ford, and Ford's wife, Bridget. He was so distracted he never read it.

Sailing without his family, William arrived in New Castle, Delaware, on October 27, then continued up the Delaware River to Philadelphia and his own Pennsbury Manor. Already the streets of Philadelphia had been planned as he had directed—in a grid, with room for gardens between the houses. The two sites had been bought from the Indians, and soon thereafter William is supposed to have signed the Great Treaty, making peace with the Lenni Lenape Indians at Shackamaxon.

King James II

*Prince William
of Orange*

Unfortunately, the need to resolve a dispute over the Pennsylvania and Maryland boundaries sent William back to England.

Nothing was done before King Charles II died. His brother took over the English throne. The new king, James II, was Roman Catholic, and William used his lifelong friendship with James to convince him to pardon English Quakers. In April 1687 and 1688, the Catholic king issued declarations of indulgence, freeing dissenters but angering the Church of England majority. In November 1688, Church and Parliament invited William III of Orange and his wife, Mary, the daughter of James II, to become the new Protestant leaders of England. James II fled to France. William Penn had supported the losing side.

The boundary dispute was shelved. William was charged with high treason. For the next three years, he didn't let people know where he lived.

By then the English in the American colonies had begun fighting the French and their Indian allies in what became known as King William's War. The other English colonies provided troops and supplies, but pacifist Pennsylvania refused. To force the colony to provide support, a royal governor took William Penn's place as head of Pennsylvania.

Finally cleared of treason in November 1693, William was at home with Guli in England when she died after a long illness. He threw himself into regaining his colony. Queen Mary granted his request, as long as he would look after Pennsylvania in person and raise troops for the war.

Still William didn't go back. He reappointed William Markham deputy governor. On March 5, 1696, William married young Hannah Callowhill.

Meanwhile, in Pennsylvania, Markham was struggling with the Assembly's refusal to provide military aid for the war. William had to go back now. Two days before his planned departure, Philip and Bridget Ford forced him to sign another paper promising them land and money if he didn't pay them what he already owed.

William, Hannah, and William's daughter Letitia arrived in Pennsylvania on December 1, 1699. There were now two thousand homes and five thousand people in Philadelphia, making the city second in size only to Boston in the colonies. By February William had coaxed the Assembly into passing laws against pirates and illegal trade.

William freed all his slaves, but made them tenants on or near his estate. On October 28, 1701, a new *Frame* gave the Assembly the right to create laws. Then rumors began that colonies with individual owners would be taken over by the Crown.

William and his family sailed for England on November 3. But the threatening bill was withdrawn, William III died, and Queen Anne, who believed in toleration, came to the throne.

Nevertheless, William remained in England. In January 1702, Philip Ford died, and Bridget presented another bill. If William didn't pay up, the documents he'd mistakenly signed would give the Ford family Pennsylvania! On November 11, 1703, William asked if the Crown would buy his colony. His terms weren't good enough, and after more than three years, the Fords won their case in the courts. At sixty-three, William was taken to debtor's prison.

With money provided by other Quakers, the debt was finally settled for 7,600 pounds. William and Hannah moved into a house in Ruscombe, Berkshire. On July 30, 1718, William Penn died. Pennsylvania continued to belong to his family until the American Revolution.

Important Dates

October 14, 1644	William Penn is born on London's Tower Hill.
1657	William hears Thomas Loe, the Quaker preacher, in Ireland.
March 1662	William is expelled from Oxford University.
1663–spring 1664	William studies with Moses Amyraut in Saumur on the Loire, France.
August 1664	William begins legal training at Lincoln's Inn, London.
February 1667	William hears Thomas Loe preach a second time and becomes a Quaker.
December 1668–July 1669	Imprisoned in the Tower of London, William writes his famous tract, *No Cross, No Crown.*
April 4, 1672	William marries Gulielma Springett, stepdaughter of the well-known Quaker Isaac Penington.
March 4, 1681	William receives the final Charter that makes him Absolute Proprietor of Pennsylvania.
April–May 1682	William and the First Adventurers set up the *Frame of Government* for Pennsylvania.
October 27, 1682	William arrives in New Castle, Delaware, on his first trip to Pennsylvania.
August 12, 1684	William returns to London to settle a boundary dispute between Pennsylvania and Maryland.
August 20, 1694	After two years under a royal governor, Pennsylvania is returned to William Penn.
March 5, 1696	William marries Hannah Callowhill.
December 1, 1699	William arrives in Philadelphia on his second trip to Pennsylvania.
November 3, 1701	William and his family return to England to prevent Pennsylvania from being taken over by the Crown.
November 11, 1703	William unsuccessfully asks the Crown to buy Pennsylvania from him.
July 30, 1718	William Penn dies in Ruscombe, Berkshire.

Author's Note

During the 1600s, religion in England was still controlled by the Crown. If you weren't a member of the established Church, or didn't believe in its ranking of bishops, priests, and deacons, you were persecuted. That was true of Roman Catholics, and of Baptists, Quakers, and especially Puritans, who wanted to get rid of the bishops and the ritual and establish stricter discipline. During the years of Cromwell and the Commonwealth, the Puritans gained control, but in general, toleration depended on who happened to be king. It wasn't until the Act of Toleration in 1689 that religious liberty began to be taken seriously in England.

William Penn had seven children with each of his two wives. Of the first seven, only two survived to become adults. Of the rest, four reached adulthood.

William returned to London from Ireland after the Great Fire of 1666. When it came time to plan Philadelphia, he remembered that experience. He insisted that there be gardens between the houses "that it may be a green country town which will never be burned, and always be wholesome."